W9-DDB-332

Learning About the

Human Body Systems

Learning About the Respiratory System

by Susan Dudley Gold

Enslow Publishers, Inc.
40 Industrial Road
Box 398
Berkeley Heights, NJ 07922
USA

http://www.enslow.com

To Maureen Leary for her dedicated
fight against tobacco and to the staff and volunteers of the
American Lung Association and all those who work to ensure that
we have clean air to breathe.

Copyright © 2013 by Susan Dudley Gold

All rights reserved.

No part of this book may be reproduced by any means without the written permission of the publisher.

Original edition published as *The Respiratory System* in 2003.

Library of Congress Cataloging-in-Publication Data

Gold, Susan Dudley.
  Learning about the respiratory system / Susan Dudley Gold.
      p. cm. — (Learning about the human body systems)
  Summary: "Learn about how the nose, throat and lungs all work together to keep us breathing"— Provided by publisher.
  Includes bibliographical references and index.
  ISBN 978-0-7660-4161-5
  1. Respiratory organs—Juvenile literature. I. Title.
  QM251.G65 2013
  611'.2—dc23

                                                  2012011104

Future editions:
Paperback ISBN: 978-1-4644-0243-2
ePUB ISBN: 978-1-4645-1158-5
PDF ISBN: 978-1-4646-1158-2

Printed in the United States of America

082012 Lake Book Manufacturing, Inc., Melrose Park, IL

10 9 8 7 6 5 4 3 2 1

To Our Readers: We have done our best to make sure all Internet addresses in this book were active and appropriate when we went to press. However, the author and the publisher have no control over and assume no liability for the material available on those Internet sites or on other Web sites they may link to. Any comments or suggestions can be sent by e-mail to comments@enslow.com or to the address on the back cover.

♻ Enslow Publishers, Inc., is committed to printing our books on recycled paper. The paper in every book contains 10% to 30% post-consumer waste (PCW). The cover board on the outside of each book contains 100% PCW. Our goal is to do our part to help young people and the environment too!

Photo Credits: © Art Explosion, Nova Development Corp, pp. 21, 40; Centers for Disease Control, p. 29; © Life Art, Williams & Wilkins, pp. 4, 7, 9, 11, 13, 14, 15; © Michael Valdez/Photos.com, p. 1; National Cancer Institute, p. 27; Paulo Cruz/Photos.com, p. 20; PhotoDisc, p. 34; Shutterstock.com, pp. 24, 36, 39; © Susan Dudley Gold, p. 19.

Cover Photo: © iStockphoto.com/Carmen Martínez Banús

Contents

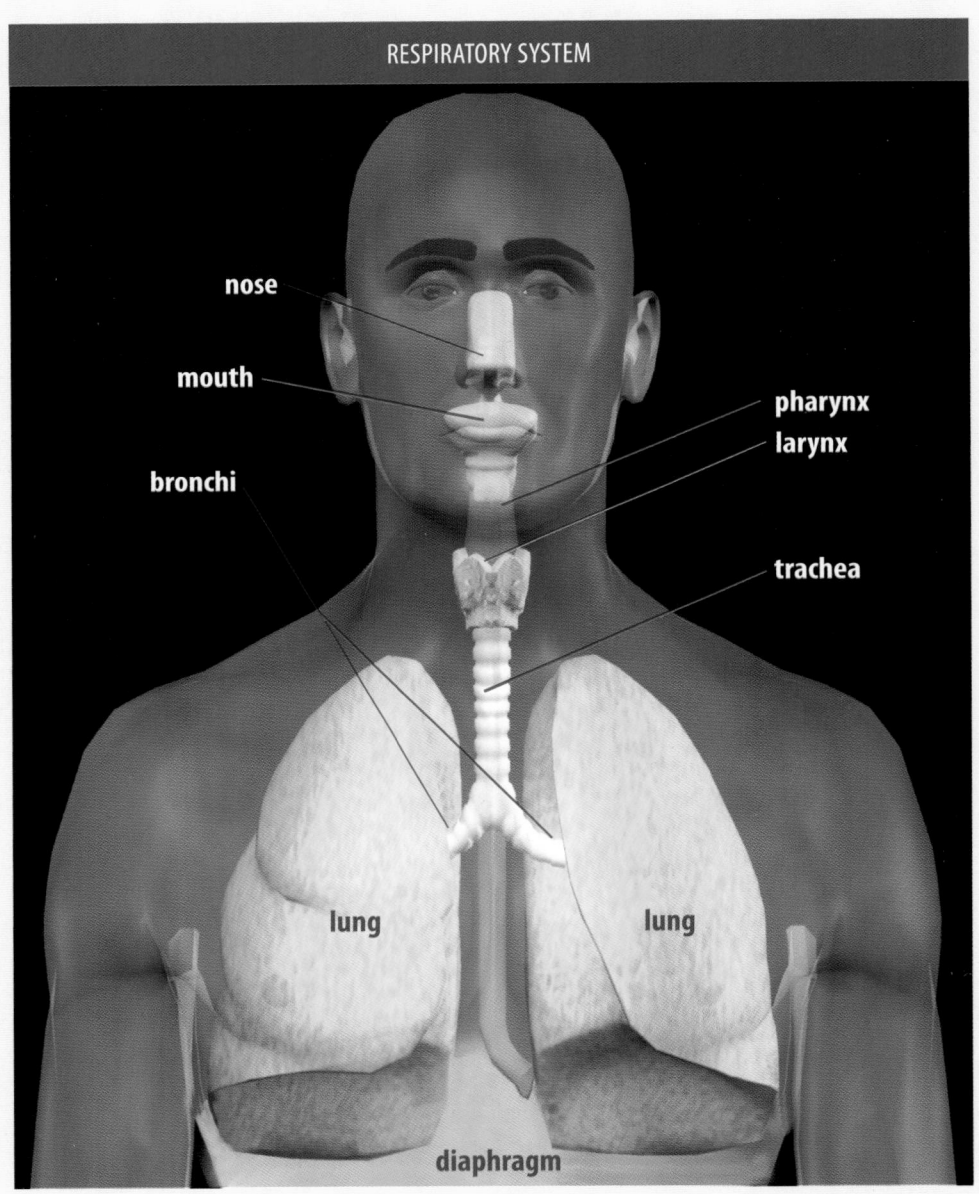

RESPIRATORY SYSTEM

nose

mouth

pharynx

larynx

bronchi

trachea

lung

lung

diaphragm

What Is the Nervous System?

Chapter 1

Jennifer Onacki celebrated her twelfth birthday by blowing out twelve candles on her birthday cake. She took a deep breath, closed her eyes and made a wish, then blew as hard as she could. The flames flickered and went out as the stream of air hit.

Throughout this book, Jennifer will serve as an example of how the **respiratory system** affects our daily lives. Without even thinking, we take a breath every few seconds and almost immediately exhale. This routine keeps us alive. A person whose breathing, or respiration, stops for long enough will die.

The mechanism people use to breathe is called the respiratory system. The nose, the throat, and the **lungs** are all part of the system. Working together, they bring **oxygen** gas into the body and expel **carbon dioxide** gas.

In addition to controlling breathing, the respiratory system helps ward off germs and poisons that might otherwise enter the body through the air. It also warms the air and adds moisture before sending the air into the lungs. Sneezing, coughing, talking, smelling, and the hiccups all involve the respiratory system.

Role of Oxygen

The air a person breathes into the lungs is rich in oxygen. Air also contains a large amount of nitrogen gas. Small amounts of other gases, germs, chemicals, smoke, and pollutants can also be found in the air we breathe.

Oxygen enables the body to use the energy in food (calories). Every cell in the body needs oxygen to do its job. When we breathe, a muscle called the **diaphragm** contracts, expanding the chest and allowing oxygen-rich air to rush in. Oxygen molecules pass through the walls of the lungs into tiny blood vessels called **capillaries**. The blood within the capillaries absorbs the oxygen and carries it to tissues throughout the body.

Sometimes a person needs more oxygen than normal. A person who is running or exercising vigorously uses more oxygen than a person who is resting. To get more oxygen to the body, a person breathes faster and takes deeper breaths. The heart beats more rapidly, speeding up the blood carrying oxygen to the body's cells. If Jennifer Onacki saw her friend across the park and ran to catch up with her, she would use a lot of energy to run. Her body would demand more oxygen. By the time she reached her friend, Jennifer would be breathing very fast indeed—panting, in fact. After resting a bit, however, she would be able to breathe normally again. When people are fearful or excited, they also require more oxygen.

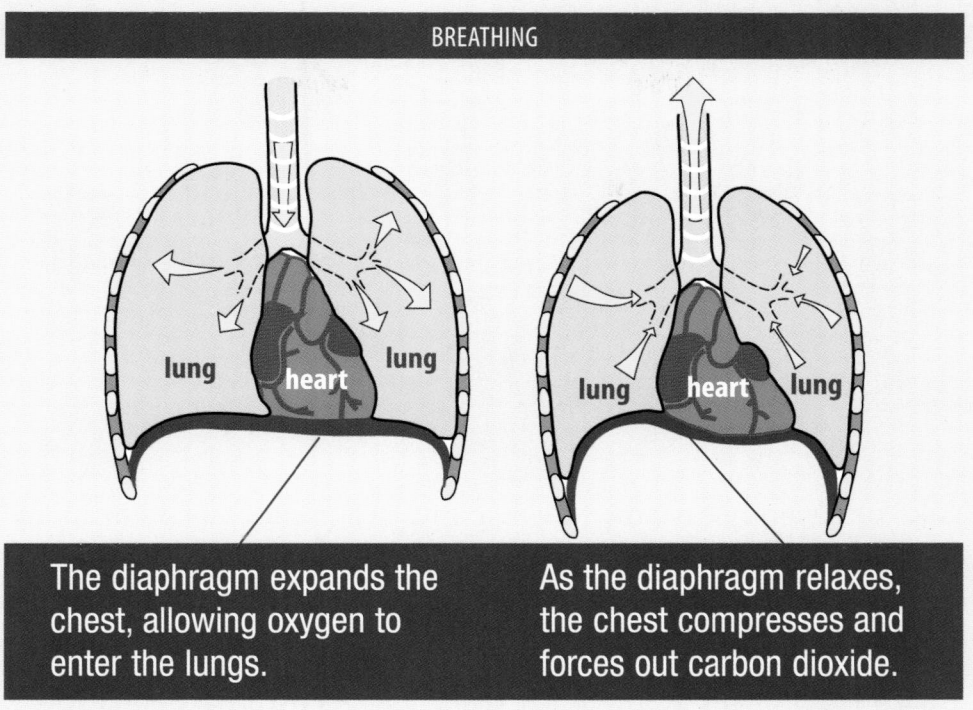

BREATHING

The diaphragm expands the chest, allowing oxygen to enter the lungs.

As the diaphragm relaxes, the chest compresses and forces out carbon dioxide.

Out with the 'Bad Air'

As oxygen enters the body's tissues, another gas—carbon dioxide—leaves the cells and flows into the capillaries. Most of the carbon dioxide dissolves in the blood, where it reacts with water to form bicarbonate. This helps keep the blood from becoming too acidic or too alkaline. The bicarbonate and any remaining carbon dioxide molecules travel in the blood to the lungs. When the diaphragm relaxes, the chest compresses, forcing out the carbon dioxide along with the rest of the used air. The cycle repeats as the person inhales, bringing in more oxygen, then exhales, expelling carbon dioxide.

Who Is on the Team?

Like other body systems, the respiratory system consists of many parts that work together. From the nose to the lungs, the parts of the respiratory system focus chiefly on getting oxygen into the body and removing carbon dioxide from the body. Each of the major parts of the respiratory "team" has its own particular job to do. They are divided into two sections: the upper respiratory tract and the lower respiratory tract. The nose and the **pharynx**, or throat, are part of the upper tract. The lower tract consists of the **larynx** (the voice box), the **trachea** (the windpipe), the bronchial system, and the lungs. All along the way, as air passes from the nose to the lungs, the different parts of the system help filter the air and work to keep germs, harmful chemicals, and pollutants away from the sensitive lungs.

Nose
The nose handles the respiratory system's first "assignment," getting air into the body. Air enters the nostrils and travels

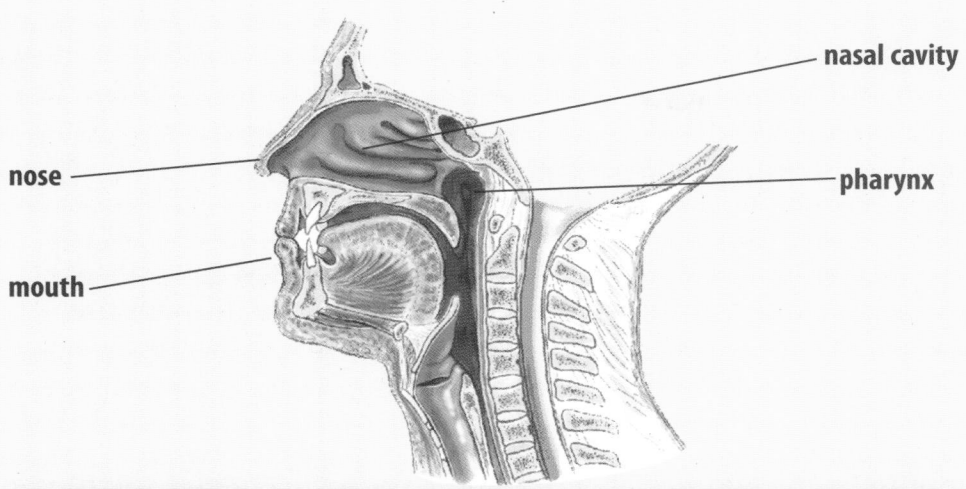

nasal cavity

nose

pharynx

mouth

UPPER RESPIRATORY TRACT
Air enters through the mouth and the nose and travels into the pharynx.

through the nasal cavity. As air passes through the nose, coarse hairs in the nostrils stop particles, germs, and other harmful substances from going to the lungs.

A mucous **membrane** lining the nasal passages secretes **mucus**, a thick fluid that traps the particles that fall from the nose hair. Embedded in the mucous membrane are tiny hair-like stalks called **cilia**. The cilia wave continually. This motion forces the mucus to flow out of the nostrils and down to the throat. By swallowing, a person moves the germ-laden mucus out of the throat and into the stomach, where acids dissolve it.

Sometimes smog or other pollutants cause a buildup of mucus in the nose, irritating the mucous membrane. When that happens, a message travels from the membrane to the brain, triggering a sneeze. The sneeze blows the excess mucus—and the offending pollutant—out the mouth and the nose.

In addition to screening out germs, the nose moistens and warms the air before it enters the lungs. The mucous membrane gives off water vapor, which the air absorbs on its way to the throat. Blood in the capillaries of the nasal passages warms the air.

When a person has a cold, the nose may become blocked by excess mucus. Then the person must breathe through the mouth. Air from the nose and the mouth goes down the trachea to the lungs. But the mouth does not have the same safeguards provided by the nose. When a person breathes through the mouth, some additional germs and cold air may enter the throat and lungs.

The nose also allows us to smell the sweetness of a rose or the mouth-watering aroma of a turkey dinner. Cells at the top of nasal passages called olfactory receptors detect chemicals in the air. A message then travels from the receptors to the brain. The brain processes the information and creates the sensation of smell.

Pharynx

After leaving the nasal passages, air enters the **pharynx** or throat. The pharynx, a tube about 5 inches (13 cm) long, funnels the air into the larynx. It provides a second layer of defense against germs. As in the nose, a mucous membrane lines the pharynx and traps germs still in the air. Tonsils in the pharynx stand guard against germs that escape the mucus. One set of tonsils, the palatine tonsils, sits on either side of the tongue, at the back of the pharynx. The lingual tonsils are located at the base of the tongue. Adenoids,

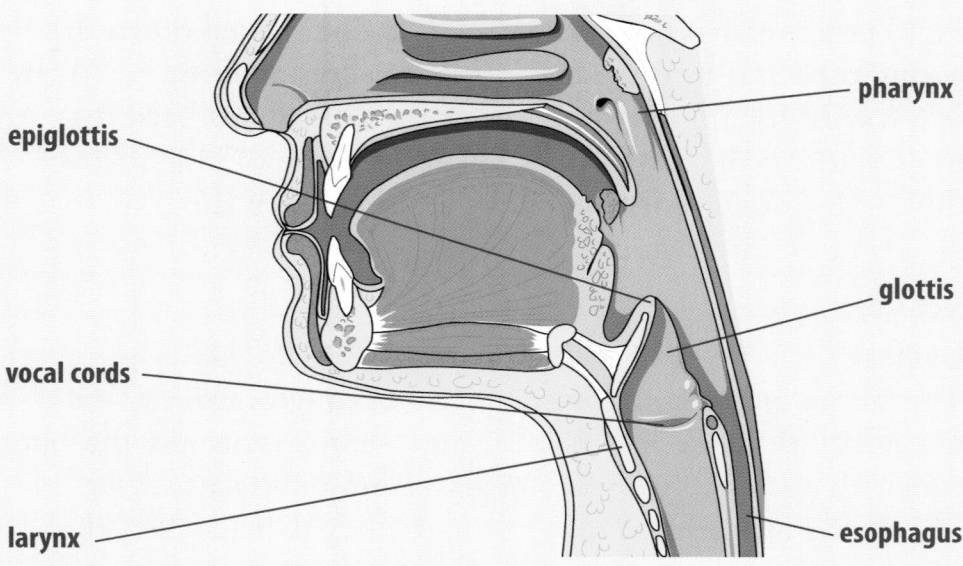

another type of tonsil, are up high to the rear of the pharynx. White blood cells in the tonsils attack germs and destroy them. Air passing through the pharynx enters the **glottis**, a small opening that leads to the larynx.

The opening to the **esophagus** is also located in the pharynx. This long, thin tube transports food and water from the pharynx to the stomach.

With two tubes opening into the pharynx, how does the body keep straight which one to use for air and which one to use for food? The body has an ingenious way of preventing a person from choking. When someone swallows, a flap of tissues called the **epiglottis** covers the glottis. This leaves only the esophagus open, and that is the path the food follows to the stomach. Sometimes, however, when a person laughs or

11

sucks in a breath while eating, food can be sucked down the wrong tube and into the larynx. This causes a person to cough as a way of forcing the food out of the larynx and back into the mouth. If the cough does not remove the food blocking the airway, the person will choke and may even die if the passage is not cleared quickly.

Larynx

The larynx, made up of several pieces of tough cartilage, lies in the center of the neck. It is a 2-inch (5-cm) passageway through which air passes between the pharynx and the trachea. Like other parts of the respiratory team, the larynx helps filter the air and protect the lungs from germs. Cilia in the larynx beat constantly, forcing the unwanted particles embedded in mucus upward to the pharynx. There they are swallowed and dissolved in stomach acid.

The larynx is also known as the voice box. This is because the vocal cords are located on either side of the larynx. These two bands of tissue enable us to speak. When the bands are stretched by muscles attached to the pieces of cartilage, the force of air exhaled from the lungs causes the vocal cords to vibrate. This vibration creates the sound of a person's voice.

The more force that is used in expelling air from the lungs, the louder the voice becomes. The vocal cords have varying pitches depending on how tight or how Relaxed the cords are. The pitch of the voice—how high or low the tone is—becomes higher as the cords are tensed.

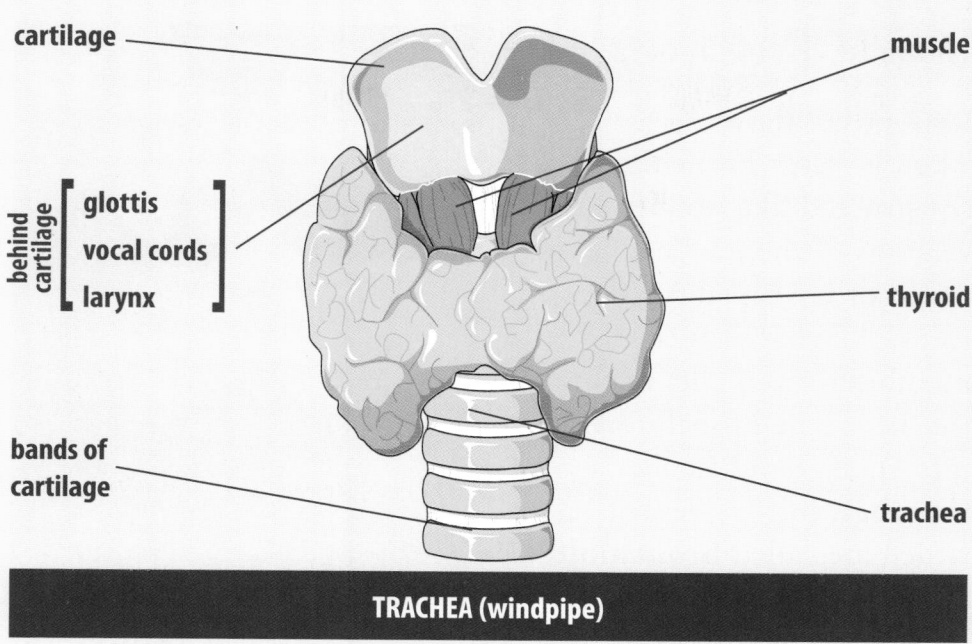

cartilage

muscle

behind cartilage
- glottis
- vocal cords
- larynx

thyroid

bands of cartilage

trachea

TRACHEA (windpipe)

Trachea

The trachea, or windpipe, continues the passage of air toward the lungs. The narrow tube measures about 5 to 6 inches long (13 to 15 cm) and begins just below the spot where the neck joins the trunk. A series of fifteen to twenty bands of cartilage, each shaped like a C, keep the trachea open and prevent it from collapsing. It, too, has a mucous membrane and cilia that filter the incoming air and sweep any remaining particles or foreign matter back up to the pharynx. At its base the trachea divides into two smaller tubes called **bronchi** (sometimes called bronchial tubes) that lead to the lungs.

Bronchi, Bronchioles, and Alveoli

The two large bronchi are constructed like smaller versions of the trachea. Composed of C-shaped cartilage rings, they have mucous membranes and cilia to filter the air. These bronchi divide into smaller and smaller branches, the smallest of which are called **bronchioles**. These bronchioles spread throughout the lungs.

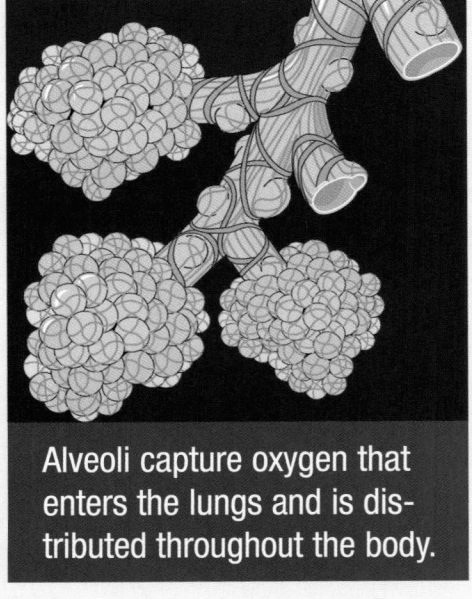

Alveoli capture oxygen that enters the lungs and is distributed throughout the body.

The whole bronchial system looks like two upside-down trees. Bands of smooth muscle ring the bronchioles. These muscles tighten and relax to regulate the amount of air that enters and leaves the lungs.

At the end of each bronchiole, millions of tiny sacs called **alveoli** fill with air. Like a fish net packed with fish, capillaries surround the alveoli and circulate blood around them. Both the alveoli and the capillaries have thin walls that make it easy for oxygen and carbon dioxide to pass through.

One more germ-fighter stands guard to ward off germs and protect the body from infection. **Macrophages**, large cells that start off as typical white blood cells, circulate among the alveoli. These cells surround and destroy germs that have managed to slip through the respiratory system's air filters.

Lungs

The lungs resemble two large balloons, each roughly the shape of a cone. But instead of simply being filled with air like a balloon, the lungs are packed with tiny alveoli, and each of these is filled with air. Each lung contains more than 300 million alveoli, grouped together in bunches like grapes. Oxygen flows through the thin walls of the alveoli. The lung's alveoli, if spread out, would cover an area about the size of a tennis court. Without these tiny air sacs, the lungs would contain only about five or six square feet of surface area. The difference is important because the greater the surface area, the more oxygen can pass through the lungs. The alveoli allow the lungs to process hundreds of times more air than would be true otherwise.

In addition to their key role in breathing, the lungs help protect the body from harmful substances and germs. Only about one-tenth of the lungs consist of tissue. The rest is filled with air and blood.

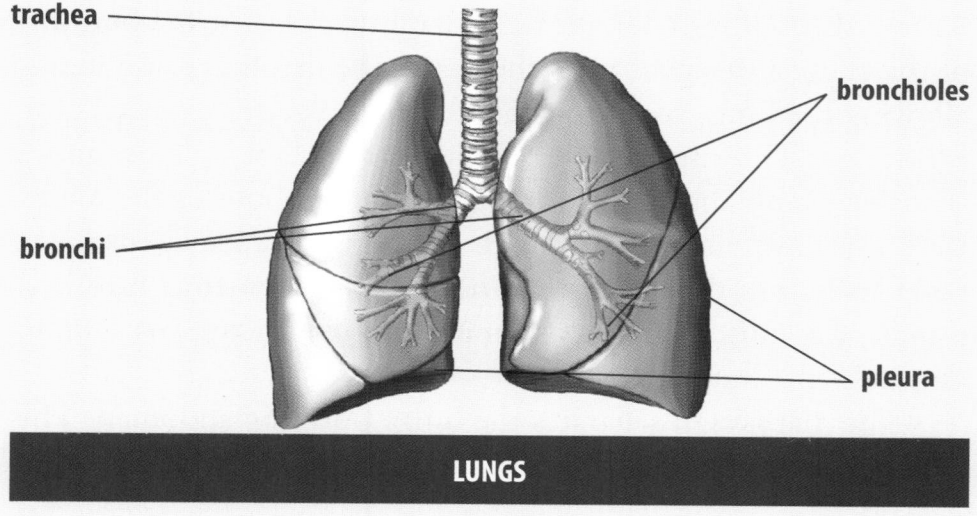

LUNGS

The lungs lie within the chest, in the **thoracic cavity**. The rib cage's twenty-four bones encircle the lungs and heart, protecting them from outside forces. The right lung is divided into three parts, or lobes. The left lung, with only two lobes, is slightly smaller to make room for the heart. Both lungs are enclosed in a waterproof, airtight sac called the **pleura**. Fluid surrounds the membranes of the pleura and keeps them moist. **Lymph nodes** help keep the lungs drained. They also assist in fighting disease. The lungs are among the body's most delicate organs. That is why the body has so many guards posted all along the way to protect the lungs. Pollution, smoking, and diseases that get through the safeguards can cause severe damage to the lungs. Exposure to smoke can turn the lungs' pink tissue black.[1]

Diaphragm

Muscles are the workhorses that power the respiratory system. A large sheet of muscle called the diaphragm lies at the bottom of the chest. On signal from the brain, the diaphragm tightens, allowing the lungs room to expand for inhalation, or relaxes for exhalation. This muscle and muscles in the chest wall also move the rib cage up and down, forcing air into and out of the lungs. Like a bellows, the lungs fill with air as the rib cage opens up and expel air as the rib cage contracts. When someone breathes rapidly, the muscles in the abdomen also contract to force more air out of the lungs.

The diaphragm separates the lungs from the abdomen. This adds another layer of protection for the lungs.

How Does the System Work?

Chapter 3

Like all parts of the body, the respiratory system receives its instructions from the brain. A cluster of nerve cells called the **respiratory center** resides in the brain stem. These nerve cells send out messages to the diaphragm and to muscles in the chest wall to tighten or contract.

The brain controls these actions automatically. The respiratory center sends out a message to the diaphragm about twelve to twenty times a minute. In response, an adult will breathe about twelve to twenty times a minute. Infants breathe much more rapidly. They usually take thirty to fifty breaths a minute.

A person will continue breathing with or without thinking about it. People can, however, control their breathing—up to a certain point. Using the cerebral cortex, the section of the brain that governs thinking, a person can override the automatic system that regulates breathing. Being able to hold one's breath for a time can save a person's life. For example, swimmers hold their breath while underwater. Not breathing in smoke or dangerous fumes can keep a person from getting sick.

But if a person holds the breath too long, the brain will take over and force the person to exhale and then begin breathing again. When a person fails to exhale, carbon dioxide collects in the blood. Too much carbon dioxide makes the blood acidic. When acid in the blood reaches a certain level, receptors in the brain stem and the neck's blood vessels send a message to the respiratory center in the brain. As soon as the message is relayed, the respiratory center resumes its job. It overrides the signals from the cerebral cortex that are interfering with breathing and sends its own signals to the body to exhale and inhale regularly.

The body has other safeguards to protect the lungs from taking in too much air and exploding like an overblown balloon. Special cells in the lungs measure how much air enters the lungs. When the lungs are full, these cells signal the respiratory center. The center then signals the muscles to stop the person from inhaling more air.

Exchanging Gases

Air, like other gases, travels from high-pressure areas to low-pressure areas. When a person's chest cavity expands, the pressure in the lungs is decreased, and air rushes in. The oxygen in the air entering the lungs seeps through the thin walls of the alveoli. From there the oxygen passes into the blood-filled capillaries surrounding the alveoli.

Once in the bloodstream, the oxygen molecules bind to molecules of **hemoglobin**, a protein in red blood cells. Each hemoglobin molecule carries four oxygen molecules through

alveoli & capillaries

Oxygen flows through the thin walls of the alveolus to the red blood cells in the capillary, while carbon dioxide from the red blood cells flows from the capillary to the alveolus.

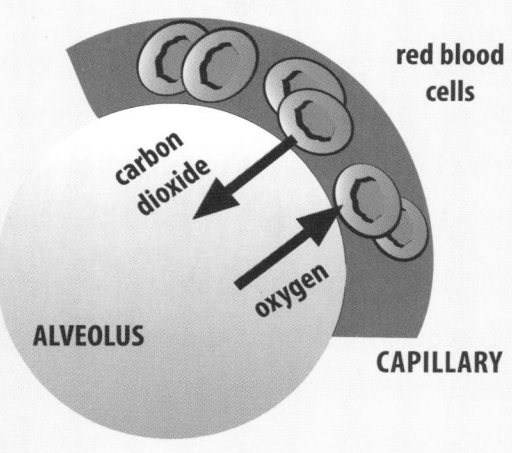

red blood cells

carbon dioxide

oxygen

ALVEOLUS

CAPILLARY

GAS EXCHANGE

the bloodstream. On average a person breathes in 2,600 to 5,300 gallons (9,800 to 20,000 liters) of air a day. From that air, the person uses about 6 pounds (2,700 grams) of oxygen daily.

When the oxygen-rich blood reaches tissue in need of oxygen, the gas flows out of the blood cells and into the tissue. If the tissue is using a lot of oxygen, a large number of hemoglobin molecules will release their store of oxygen.

In turn, carbon dioxide in the tissue enters the blood. Most of the carbon dioxide dissolves in the blood. The remaining carbon dioxide binds to empty hemoglobin molecules and is carried back toward the lungs. There it enters the capillaries and alveoli to be exhaled as waste gas. The cycle repeats itself with each breath a person takes.

This kind of process, in which one gas flows one way as another flows the opposite way, is called a **gas exchange**. Each exchange between oxygen and carbon dioxide gases takes only a fraction of a second.

The lungs provide a continuous supply of oxygen to the body. This allows us to breathe regularly without a pause—even when we are using much more oxygen than we normally do. When we run, for example, we breathe more rapidly and take deeper breaths and our heart beats faster. This forces blood to travel quickly through the lungs, where it retrieves all the oxygen needed.

Something to Talk About

The respiratory system also plays an important role in speech. Remember our friend Jennifer? If she called to her friends, the vocal cords in her larynx would vibrate. This helps produce the sound of her voice. The two vocal cords located in the center of the larynx are made of connective tissue. They are attached to a piece of cartilage in back of

Jennifer talks to a friend on the telephone. Her vocal cords vibrate to help produce the sound of her voice.

VOCAL CORDS

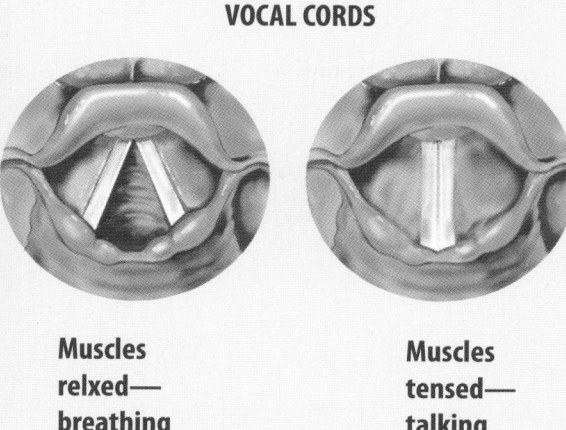

When a person breathes, two pieces of cartilage in the center of the larynx separate. The vocal muscles pull the pieces together when a person talks.

Muscles relxed— breathing

Muscles tensed— talking

each of the vocal cords. When a person breathes in, the pieces of cartilage separate. This opens the passage to the bronchi, and air rushes into the lungs.

When Jennifer talks, she exhales at the same time she tenses the vocal muscles. This stretches the vocal cords and pulls them closer together. The exhaled air is partially blocked by the smaller opening that is now between the two pieces of cartilage. As the air pushes against the opening, pressure builds until finally a burst of air escapes. As the air passes over the stretched vocal cords, they vibrate, creating sound. Not all sounds are produced this way, however. Some—like the "f" and the "s" sounds—are created by air as it travels through the mouth.

To make her voice louder, Jennifer must increase the force of the air passing through the opening between the vocal cords. The stronger the burst of air, the louder Jennifer's shouts become.

Chapter 4

Under Attack

As we have seen, the respiratory system has a good defense network to protect the lungs. Even with all that in place, germs and harmful substances sometimes get through. When they do, they can cause major health problems. The lungs are particularly sensitive to pollution and smoke from cigarettes and cigars. Diseases and disorders ranging from **cancer** to colds can affect the lungs. They can interfere with gas exchange, block airways, or scar lung tissue.

Diseases and disorders that affect the lungs can cause minor irritation or life-threatening situations. A week before her birthday, Jennifer Onacki had the sniffles. They soon developed into a full-blown cold. She coughed and sneezed. Her nose was stuffed up, and her sinuses hurt. Jennifer worried that she wouldn't be able to enjoy her birthday party. She went to bed early and drank plenty of water and juice. A week later she felt fine.

Jennifer's mother helps care for elderly people in a home for those who are too ill to take care of themselves. A man who once lived there caught the flu. Because the man was old and ill already, his body could not fight off the germs that caused the flu.

He became weaker. Finally, with no strength left, he contracted bacterial **pneumonia**, a serious lung disease, and died soon after.

Because lungs perform such a vital task, any disease or disorder that affects them can be potentially dangerous. One in six deaths in the United States results from lung disease. Nearly 400,000 Americans die from lung disease each year. Breathing problems and lung disease claim the lives of more babies under one year old than any other cause. In addition, chronic lung disease—a health problem that lasts a long time, sometimes for life—plagues more than 35 million Americans.[1]

Colds and the Flu

We are surrounded by germs. These bacteria and **viruses** float unseen in the air, reside on countertops, and stick to our skin and hands. The warm, moist nasal passages provide a perfect home for viruses that cause colds. When a cold virus invades, it destroys the cells of the membranes that line the nose. This alerts the body's **immune system**, which sends an army of cells to fight off the invader. With all the new cells in the area, the nasal membranes swell. This is why Jennifer's nose felt stuffy when she had a cold. The flow of mucus also increases, causing the nose to run. The infection from a cold can affect the sinuses, the lower respiratory tract, and the middle ear. Usually colds are not serious. In most cases, the body fights off the germs within a week.

The flu also develops from a virus. It affects many parts of the body, including parts of the respiratory system. If flu germs attack the respiratory tract, the lining becomes swollen and inflamed. People with the flu may have a fever, aches, chills, a cough, and nausea.

Usually a normally healthy person can fight off a cold within a week. Getting plenty of rest and drinking lots of fluids can help.

Like colds, the flu usually goes away within a week. But for people who are already ill and those with respiratory diseases or diabetes, the flu can be dangerous. It weakens the body and makes it less able to fight off other germs. One result is that the person can develop pneumonia, as the elderly man in the home did. Antibiotics—medications that fight bacteria—can often cure pneumonia that is caused by bacteria. But antibiotics have no effect on colds, the flu, and pneumonia that is caused by a virus.

Chronic Obstructive Pulmonary Disease

Chronic obstructive pulmonary disease (COPD) includes both **emphysema** and chronic **bronchitis**. Both diseases restrict breathing and develop gradually over time. ("Pulmonary" means anything related to the lungs.)

In emphysema, the alveoli's thin walls break down. This causes breathing problems and limits the amount of oxygen the body receives. A person with emphysema will often feel breathless. Once the alveoli have been damaged, they cannot be repaired. Four million Americans have been diagnosed with emphysema. Most cases of are caused by smoking, but approximately five percent of cases occur because the person is born without enough of a certain protein (alpha 1-antitrypsin) that is needed for healthy lungs. The disease has also been linked to infection and to exposure to smog.[2]

Chronic bronchitis occurs when the bronchial tubes become inflamed over and over again. As a result, the bronchial tubes produce too much mucus. This creates a haven where germs can grow. In addition, the bronchial lining thickens and partially blocks the air flow. People with chronic bronchitis cough continually to get rid of the excess mucus. In most cases, smoking is to blame for the repeated inflammation. Viruses, bacteria, air pollution, and allergies can also lead to chronic bronchitis. 9.5 million people in the United States were diagnosed with chronic bronchitis in 2006. If it is not treated, chronic bronchitis can cause permanent damage to the lungs.[3]

Medical researchers estimate between 80 and 90 percent of all cases of COPD are the result of smoking. COPD is the fourth leading cause of death in the United States. It was estimated that 127,000 people died in 2005 due to the disease and its complications.[4]

Asthma and Other Respiratory Problems

Asthma occurs when smoke, pollen, or other substances irritate the membranes lining the bronchial tubes. Responding to the irritation, the body's immune system sends an army of white blood cells to the site. This action causes the membranes to swell. With all the inflammation, the airways to the lungs become clogged. In addition, the bronchial muscles contract. This makes it hard for the person to breathe.

Asthma is a chronic condition. It can be triggered by **allergens**, substances that cause an allergic reaction in some people. Infections, exercise, cold air, fumes, or chemicals in the workplace can also bring on an asthma attack. In the United States, 26 million people have been diagnosed with asthma. Many more Americans may have the disease but have not been diagnosed. Asthma attacks don't usually cause permanent damage, but repeated attacks can cause scarring of the bronchial tubes. People can die from asthma if they are not treated for the disease. At least 3,000 Americans die each year from asthma.

The immune system is also involved in hay fever and other allergies that are brought on by pet dander, food, pollen, dust, and a number of other substances. The white blood cells' response to these allergens causes a runny nose, watering eyes, sneezing, or other reactions such as rashes. An allergic person can also have asthma-like symptoms—clogged airways and tightened bronchial muscles—that make it difficult to breathe. Avoiding the substance that causes the allergy is the best way to deal with such symptoms. Certain medications can also help ease the symptoms triggered by allergens.

Lung Cancer

Cancer comes in many different forms. It occurs when the body's cells begin to divide rapidly. This out-of-control growth can cause tumors, or lumps, to grow in the body. The cancer may spread, interfering with the body's functions and eventually causing death if the cancer is not controlled.

A person can get lung cancer by breathing in smoke or other cancer-causing agents over a period of time. This may cause abnormal cells to form in the lining of the bronchi or bronchioles. If exposure to such toxins continues, more abnormal cells form. These cells can become cancerous, form tumors, and spread throughout the body.

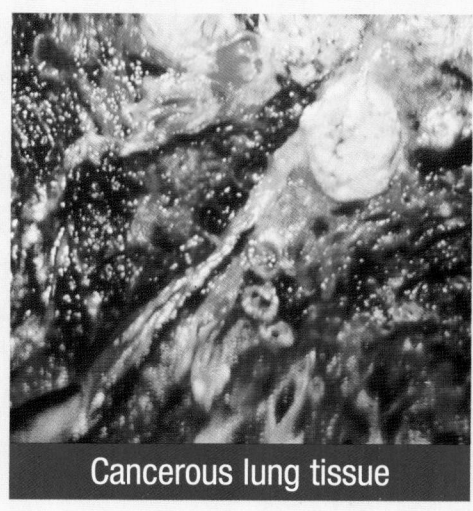

Cancerous lung tissue

More people die from lung cancer than any other type of cancer. In the year 2007, more than 160,000 Americans died from lung cancer.[5] As in COPD and other lung ailments, most cases of lung cancer—between 80 and 90 percent—are caused by smoking. People who don't smoke but live with someone who does or are exposed to smoke in other ways can also die from the disease. An estimated 3,400 people die each year from lung cancer caused by "secondhand smoke."[6]

Radon gas, a colorless, odorless gas that comes from soil—especially soil found under buildings—is blamed for most other cases of lung cancer. Nearly one in every fifteen American homes has an unhealthy level of radon. Because the gas cannot be seen, a special test kit must be used to measure the amount of radon in a building. Special fans can be installed to blow radon out of homes, schools, and other sites with too much of the gas.

Dangerous fumes from certain jobs can also cause lung cancer. People who work with asbestos, uranium, arsenic, and certain other substances are at a greater risk of developing lung disease.

Pneumonia and Tuberculosis

Pneumonia is an infection of the lungs that can be fatal. It can be caused by viruses, bacteria, or other agents that infect the lungs. Pneumonia can also occur when a person breathes in fumes, food, or other substances that cause the lungs to become inflamed. Some diseases, like **tuberculosis** (TB), can also lead to pneumonia.

In pneumonia, fluid collects in the alveoli and interferes with their ability to hold oxygen and carbon dioxide. Because of this, people with the disease have a hard time breathing.

Pneumonia caused by bacteria or fungi can be treated with antibiotic medication. (Fungi include yeast, mold, and certain other plantlike material that, if breathed in, can infect the lungs.) Viral pneumonia generally is less severe, and in most cases people heal on their own.

A specific germ, or bacterium, causes tuberculosis. When a person with tuberculosis coughs or sneezes, it propels the germ through the air. A healthy person can breathe in the germ when he or she inhales. But it takes many germs to become infected. Even when a person becomes infected with TB germs, he or she may not become sick. The body's immune system fights off the germs. If the body cannot destroy the TB germs, the person develops the disease.

TB germs attack the lungs. Sometimes other organs and tissues can also be affected. The infection can destroy lung tissue and other areas if it is not treated. People with TB used to have to live in special hospitals for months, even years. Today, antibiotic medications have greatly reduced the number of

TB cases in the United States. But recently, new strains of the disease have developed that don't respond to the medications used in the past. Researchers are working on new treatments to combat the disease. TB remains a major health problem in

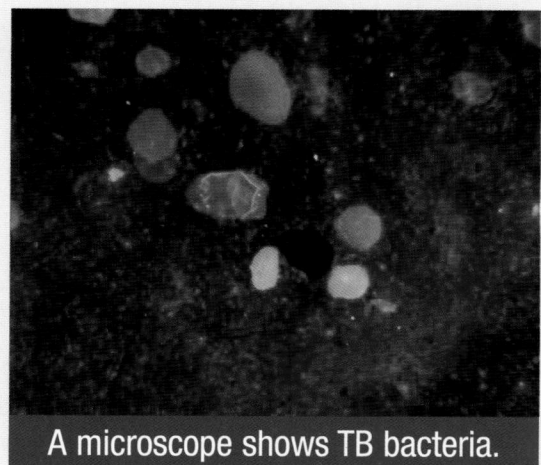

A microscope shows TB bacteria.

other parts of the world, particularly Africa. In 2010 there were more than 8.8 million new cases of TB, and 1.46 million deaths from the disease worldwide.[7]

Cystic Fibrosis

In cystic fibrosis, mucus that forms in the respiratory system is much thicker than normal. The thick mucus blocks the airways leading to the lungs and makes it difficult to breathe. The mucus also collects germs, which can infect the lungs and damage them forever. With each infection, the lungs become more scarred, making it even harder to breathe. Therapy that shakes or pounds the back can dislodge the thick mucus. By coughing, the person can force the mucus up the throat and into the mouth, where it can be spit out. Cystic fibrosis occurs when a person is born with a certain flawed gene inherited from both parents.

Anthrax

Anthrax is caused by a bacterium called *Bacillus anthracis*. The bacterium gives off spores, tiny substances that can cling to the skin or to food or that a person can inhale. Most cases of anthrax in humans come from sheep and other farm animals. It is very rare.

In the fall of 2001, anthrax spores were placed in letters addressed to American politicians and celebrities in what was later determined by the FBI to be a criminal act. Five Americans died as a result of these acts. It was the first case of inhalation anthrax in the United States since 1978. In most cases, a person must inhale thousands of anthrax spores to develop inhalation anthrax. The germs attack the respiratory system and break down the blood vessels in the lungs. At first, a person has symptoms similar to the flu. Later, the person has difficulty breathing. Antibiotics can help combat the germs if taken early enough—a few days after contracting inhalation anthrax. The skin form of anthrax is less serious and can be treated in the first few weeks with antibiotics.

Effects of Smoking and Pollution

A burning cigarette emits more than 2,000 substances. Many of these are harmful to the body. Among the most dangerous are carbon monoxide, formaldehyde, ammonia, and sulfur dioxide. These chemicals can change the structure of cells in the lungs, leading to cancer. They can cause swelling and inflame lung tissue, symptoms of chronic bronchitis. They also upset the delicate balance of chemicals and proteins in the body. This leads to the destruction of tissue, which can cause emphysema. Smoking also slows the action of cilia in the respiratory tract. Because of the slowdown, smokers—and those exposed to smoke—are more at risk from germs and other irritants that may enter the lungs.

Smoking can cause several respiratory ailments, including chronic bronchitis, emphysema, and lung cancer.

Pollutants are another common cause of respiratory problems. Practically every month, it seems, new products come on the market. Like other Americans, Jennifer Onacki's family uses many of these products in their everyday life. Their car, equipped with airbags and plastic cup holders, takes them to work and school. They use "new and improved" spray cleaners on their carpets to remove grime and dirt. They store leftovers in plastic containers designed to keep food fresher. All of these things make life easier for Jennifer and her family.

But many advances have come at the expense of the environment. Emissions from cars and trucks turn fresh air into smog. Smokestacks at plants making plastics emit toxic gases into the air. Incinerators burning trash spew ash and chemicals into the atmosphere. Inside our houses, cleaning fluids, carpets, air fresheners, and other materials give off unhealthy fumes. Repeated exposure to these harmful substances can affect the lungs. Pollutants have been linked to a number of health problems, including asthma.

Staying Healthy

People who have smoked and stop are much less likely to get lung cancer or other lung diseases than people who continue to smoke. Healthy new cells gradually replace the cells affected by smoking. The risk of lung cancer in people who once smoked is reduced by as much as half after ten years of not smoking. Remember, though, the best way to keep lungs healthy is not to smoke at all.

People can also protect their lungs by avoiding toxic fumes and secondhand smoke. Jennifer's parents don't allow anyone to smoke in their home. That protects the family from secondhand smoke that could damage their lungs. Many states have passed laws banning smoking in public buildings. Some areas also forbid smoking in restaurants and other places where people gather.

Air pollution can also harm the lungs. Cars and trucks and industrial plants that burn coal or oil discharge dangerous chemicals. These chemicals mix with sunlight to form smog. Like smoke from a cigarette, smog can irritate the lungs. It causes membranes to become inflamed and can trigger asthma attacks. At times, smog becomes so thick in some cities that people have to wear masks in order to breathe.

Cleaning the Air

As more people drove cars, opened factories, and ran energy plants, air pollution in the twentieth century grew severe. The Air Pollution Control Act of 1955 became the first in a series of federal laws passed by Congress to reduce air pollution. The Clean Air Act of 1963, amended in 1965, 1966, 1967, 1969, 1970, and 1990, followed with rules limiting fumes from power plants, mills and factories, cars, and other sources.

Reducing air pollution is one way to help people stay healthy.

In recent years, indoor air pollution has become more of a problem. Modern buildings, sealed tightly against the elements, trap chemicals emitted from cleaning solutions, paint, carpets, and other materials. Levels of some pollutants have been found to be twice as high indoors as outdoors. In a few cases, pollutant levels were 100 times higher inside than outside. To protect the lungs from these hazardous fumes, rooms need to be properly ventilated. Workers exposed to dangerous chemicals on the job are required to wear masks that filter out the fumes. Even so, these workers tend to develop more respiratory ailments than other people.

Healthy Body, Healthy Lungs

Keeping the body healthy by exercising, eating nutritious foods, and drinking plenty of water can also help protect the lungs. A healthy body has a healthy immune system, which can fight off many of the germs that threaten the lungs. If the body is weakened by disease or other health problems, the immune system may not be able to resist germs that cause lung disease.

Antibiotics and other drugs have saved many lives by killing germs infecting the lungs. People with asthma have been able to prevent attacks by using medications on a regular basis.

Some diseases, like cystic fibrosis, can damage the lungs so badly that the person cannot breathe on his or her own. Doctors can replace a diseased lung with a healthy lung from a person who has recently died. In some cases, doctors transplant only a piece, or lobe, of a lung from a living person, usually a family member. The lobe will grow and take on much of the work of the lung, allowing the ill person to breathe much more easily. Transplants are risky, though. The person who receives the transplant must undergo major surgery. He or she must also take medication to prevent the body from rejecting the new lung. If the transplant is taken from a living person, then that person also faces major surgery and a fairly long recovery period.

Essential Duties

Most of the time, we hardly give our respiratory system a thought. But when we cannot breathe for some reason, we realize in a hurry how important the system is. Like the gas tank that pumps gasoline to run our cars, the respiratory system brings in the fuel that unlocks the energy we need to survive. Without it, we would not last long.

Knowing the important duties performed by the respiratory system, we must work to protect the air we breathe. What can one person do? There are many steps you can take to promote healthy lungs—for yourself and for those around you. Here are some suggestions:

Cover your mouth whenever you cough or sneeze.

◆ Cover your mouth when you cough or sneeze. Stay away from people who have colds or the flu. Wash your hands thoroughly after being exposed to cold and flu germs and before eating.

◆ Don't smoke. Encourage people who do smoke to quit. Stay out of smoky places.

◆ Test for radon in your home. If the gas exceeds healthy limits, a special fan can help get rid of radon.

◆ Use public transportation and car pools. Limit unnecessary trips in the car.

◆ Recycle plastic and other materials.

◆ Make sure rooms are well-ventilated.

- Avoid harmful sprays, dusts, and chemicals.
- Wear a mask to protect your lungs if you work with irritating substances.
- Consult a doctor if you have a chronic cough or other health problems.
- Support anti-pollution laws.

Everyone can do something to ensure cleaner air. After all, we all have to breathe!

Chapter 6

Amazing but True

Babies' lungs contain 20 million tiny air sacs (alveoli). An adult lung contains more than 300 million.[1]

Each lung in an adult weighs about one pound (2.2 kilograms).

If stretched in a straight line, the lungs' capillaries would extend almost 1,000 miles (1,600 kilometers).

The walls of the alveoli and capillaries, where gas exchange occurs, are fifty times thinner than tissue paper.[2]

Cilia, the hairlike structures that help keep the respiratory system clean, beat 1,200 times every minute.[3]

There are about 30,000 bronchioles, no thicker than a hair, in each lung.[4]

A person loses about a pint of water a day through breathing.

Air expelled during a cough travels at up to 60 miles per hour. The fastest air speed during a sneeze has been clocked at more than 100 miles per hour, as fast as the winds of some tornadoes.[5]

The diaphragm is usually to blame for hiccups. Eating too fast or other action can irritate the diaphragm and cause it to tense up suddenly. Most cases of hiccups end after a few minutes, but sometimes they can last for days.

By 2030, smoking will result in more deaths worldwide—an estimated 10 million per year—than any other cause, according to the World Bank.[6]

SNEEZE WEED

Each individual stalk of ragweed, a plant that causes severe allergic reactions in many people, produces about 1 billion pollen grains a year. The grains, blown by the wind, can travel up to 400 miles away from the original plant.

DUST MITES
Dust mites that irritate the respiratory tract feed on dead human skin. They live in mattresses, blankets, pillows, and other areas that come in contact with the skin. A mattress may contain up to 200,000 of these mites.

Tobacco use costs America an estimated $193 billion in medical costs and lost productivity per year.

Asthma causes more children to miss school than any other health problem. Children in the United States miss more than 10 million school days a year due to asthma.[7]

Dr. Joel Cooper performed the first successful lung transplant on a human in Toronto in 1983. The patient, Tom Hall, lived for seven years after the surgery.

Chapter Notes

Chapter Two: Who Is on the Team?

1. Division of Lung Diseases, National Heart, Lung, and Blood Institute, National Institutes of Health, *The Lungs in Health and Disease* (Bethesda, Md.: NIH Publications, 1997), pp. 3–7.

Chapter Four: Under Attack

1. "Lung Disease Data: 2008," American Lung Association, 2008, <http://www.lungusa.org/assets/documents/publications/lung-disease-data/LDD_2008.pdf> (January 20, 2012).
2. Ibid.
3. Ibid.
4. Ibid.
5. Ibid.
6. "Second-hand Smoke," American Cancer Society, n.d., <http://www.cancer.org/Cancer/CancerCauses/TobaccoCancer/secondhand-smoke> (January 20, 2012).
7. "Global Tuberculosis Control," World Health Organization, 2011, <http://www.who.int/tb/publications/global_report/2011/gtbr11_full.pdf> (January 23, 2012).

Chapter Six: Amazing but True

1. David M. Orenstein, *Cystic Fibrosis: A Guide for Patient and Family*, Second Edition (New York: Lippincott-Raven Publishers, 1997).

2. Division of Lung Diseases, National Heart, Lung, and Blood Institute, National Institutes of Health, *The Lungs in Health and Disease*, p. 7.

3. Orenstein.

4. "Your Lungs and Respiratory System," The Nemours Foundation, n.d., <http://kidshealth.org/kid/htbw/lungs.html#> (January 24, 2012).

5. British Broadcasting Corp., "The Guide to Life, the Universe and Everything," n.d., <http://www.bbc.co.uk/dna/hub/A876864> (January 23, 2012).

6. "A global smoking battle," *BBC News*, Aug. 2, 2000. "Tobacco Use: Targeting the Nation's Leading Killer," Centers for Disease Control and Prevention, 2011, <http://www.cdc.gov/chronicdisease/resources/publications/aag/osh.htm> (January 24, 2012)

7. "Asthma Prevalence, Health Care Use, and Mortality: United States, 2005–2009," National Center for Health Statistics, 2011, <http://www.cdc.gov/nchs/data/nhsr/nhsr032.pdf> (January 20, 2012).

Glossary

allergen—A normally harmless substance that causes an overreaction in a person with an allergy to that substance.

alveoli—Tiny sacs in the lungs where the exchange of oxygen and carbon dioxide occurs.

asthma—A respiratory disorder that temporarily narrows the airways and causes wheezing and shortness of breath.

bronchi—The larger airways within the lungs. Also called bronchial tubes.

bronchioles—Smaller airways that branch off from bronchi.

bronchitis—Inflammation of the bronchi.

cancer—Uncontrolled growth of abnormal cells.

capillaries—Tiny blood vessels with very thin walls.

carbon dioxide—Colorless, naturally occurring gas exhaled by the lungs; it can be dangerous in high concentrations.

chronic obstructive pulmonary disease (COPD)—Lung disease that restricts breathing; includes both emphysema and chronic bronchitis.

cilia—Tiny hairlike stalks that wave constantly to filter out contaminants that enter the body.

diaphragm—The large sheet of muscle that lies between the lungs and the abdomen.

emphysema—Lung disease that destroys the alveoli walls.

epiglottis—Flap of tissues that covers the glottis when a person swallows to prevent food from entering the lungs.

esophagus—Tube in the pharynx through which food passes into the stomach.

gas exchange—In respiration, the transfer of oxygen from the air to the blood and carbon dioxide from the blood to the lungs, where it is exhaled.

glottis—Opening leading to the larynx.

hemoglobin—A protein in the red blood cells that carries oxygen molecules.

immune system—The body's defense system.

larynx—Short airway connecting the pharynx and trachea; also called the voice box because it contains the vocal cords.

lungs—Two cone-shaped organs in the chest responsible for breathing.

lymph nodes—Small organs containing fluid that help fight off disease. They also help drain fluids from the lungs.

macrophages—A type of white blood cell that attacks invading germs.

membrane—Thin layer of tissue, often around an organ.

mucus—Thick fluid that coats and protects the respiratory system and other parts of the body.

oxygen—Odorless, colorless gas that unleashes energy from food; essential for life.

pharynx—The throat.

pleura—Airtight, waterproof membrane enclosing the lungs.

pneumonia—Disease in which the lungs become inflamed.

respiratory center—A cluster of nerve cells in the brain stem that instructs the respiratory system to breathe.

respiratory system—Collection of organs and related parts that bring in oxygen from the air and expel carbon dioxide.

thoracic cavity—Area in the chest where the lungs and heart are located.

trachea—Air tube that connects the larynx and the bronchi; also called the windpipe.

tuberculosis—Disease caused by bacteria that can destroy lung tissue if not treated.

virus—Substance that grows and multiplies in living things, causing infection.

Further Reading

Books

Alton, Steve. *Blood and Goo and Boogers Too!: A Heart-Pounding Pop-Up Guide to the Circulatory and Respiratory Systems.* New York: Dial Books for Young Readers, 2008.

Burstein, John. *The Remarkable Respiratory System: How Do My Lungs Work?* New York: Crabtree Pub., 2009.

Simon, Seymour. *Lungs: Your Respiratory System.* New York: Collins, 2007.

Tieck, Sarah. *Respiratory System.* Edina, Minn.: ABDO Pub., 2011.

Internet Addresses

American Lung Association
<http://www.lung.org/your-lungs/>

The Nemours Foundation. "Looking at Your Lungs," KidsHealth.
<http://kidshealth.org/kid/htbw/lungs.html>

Index